POPSY ™ in

Ballet My Way

By Tammy Laframboise

Illustrations by Steve Bermundo

Book Design by Jayme LaForest

Raspberry

Books

Raspberry

Books

Published in the United States by Raspberry Books.
ISBN-13: 978-0-9848749-0-3

Manufactured in the United States of America

To Ava, my little inspiration
And to Jayme, a standing ovation
-T.L.

To all aspiring dancers, both young and old
-S.B.

Hi, my name is Popsy
And I love to dance Ballet
I bet you'd love it too
If you tried Ballet my way

"Bal-Lay"

I like to make up stories
To help me remember my steps
Like grand battement and relevé
And turning pirouettes!

"Grrrawnd-Bot-Maw"

"Reh-Le-Vay"

"Peer-Oh-Wet"

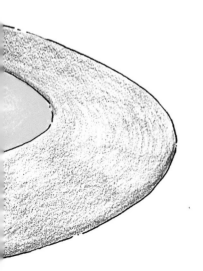

When I place my hand upon the barre
And stand up very tall
I'm like a tree with deep, deep roots
That will not let me fall

"Bar"

In first position my heels are kissing
Because they are so in love
My toes are pointed to the sides
Like the wings of a flying dove

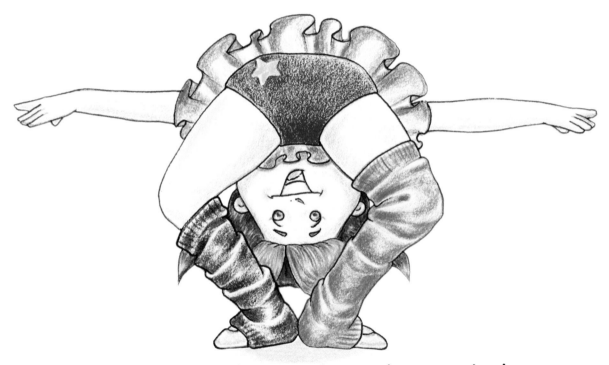

I bend my knees to make a window
That's how I do plié
I say peek-a-boo...

then close it up
Cause it's quite chilly today!

"Plee-Ay"

Relevé puts me on my toes
To reach the very top shelf

"Reh-Le-Vay"

Then I come down, my heels touch the ground
And I am so proud of myself!

When I tendu I point my toes
As pretty as can be
I can point to the front, the
side or back...

One

Two

Three

"Tawn-Doo"

I circle my leg round and round
That's called rond de jambe
Like stirring a pot of chicken soup
In the kitchen with my mom!

"Rrrohn-Duh-Jawmb"

Now it's time for grand battement
And I'm really starting to sweat
But I stand up tall and kick real high
Like a Radio City ROCK ETTE!

"Grrrawnd-Bot-Maw"

To passé my toes touch my knee
And make a pointy letter P
Try not to wiggle or wobble
Focus is the key

"Paw-Say"

Next I'll do my port de bras
And move my arms from low to high
Like blowing up a big balloon
Then...

"Por-De-Braw"

they fall to my sides

To pirouette I do passé
And spin all the way around
Like a princess at the royal ball
Wearing a beautiful crown.

"Peer-Oh-Wet"

When I sauté I bend my knees then...

JUMP

J U

JUMP
M P

I think of a quiet little mouse
And try not to land with a
THUMP!

"So-Tay"

Glissade means to glide
So I pretend to skate
Across the floor so gracefully
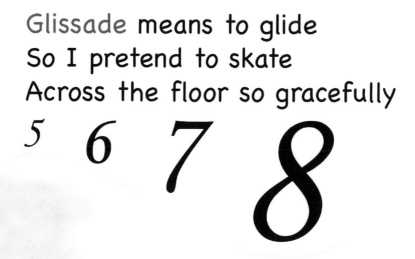

"Glee-Sawd"

Now I tippy toe so quick
That's how I do bourrée
I move so smooth across the floor
that my teacher says...

"HOORAY!

"Boo-Ray"

When I do my arabesque
I make a line so far
From my toes right to my fingertips
Then wish upon a star!

"Air-A-Besk"

Now I've practiced all my steps
Plié, tendu **and** rond de jambe,
Passé, arabesque, glissade, sauté
And grand battements.

"So-Tay"

"Plee-Ay"

"Tawn-Doo"

"Rrrohn-Duh-Jawmb"

"Air-A-Besk"

"Paw-Say"

"Glee-Sawd"

"Grrrawnd-Bot-Maw"

Relevé, pirouette, bourrée and of course
My port de bras
So now there's one thing left to do
And that's called révérence

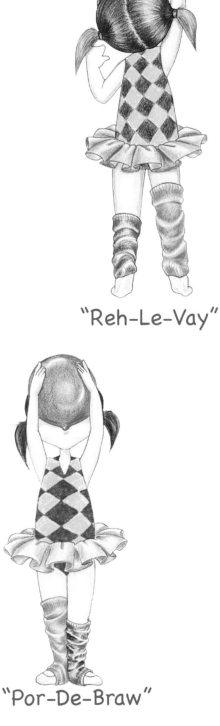

"Reh-Le-Vay"

"Peer-Oh-Wet"

"Boo-Ray"

"Por-De-Braw"

So I hold my skirt and point my toe
And bow my head TADA...

"Ray-Vay-Rawnse"

Then stand up straight and blow a kiss
To all my fans...

MUAH!!!

A very special thank you to Jayme LaForest, James Vela and Angie Ohman for their hard work in making this book become a reality. Also, to Steve Bermundo for putting the pictures in my head on paper and helping to bring Popsy to life. Thank you to my Mom, Dad and Jim for providing me with the opportunity to dance. And to my dance teachers, Nancy Pattison, Cindy Pattison-Rivard and Teresa McMillan, for providing me with the skills to follow my dreams.

All of your support means the world to me.

To purchase additional copies of this book or other books starring Popsy please visit
www.createspace.com/3677193

15235539R00026

Made in the USA
Charleston, SC
24 October 2012